What people are saying about *Thriving At Work*

"My life has been transformed by reading *Thriving At Work*. I no longer cry every morning feeling like I am driving myself willingly to prison. I now know that my job is toxic, not me... I have choices about how I can keep myself safe and feel more in control at my job."

James, Survivor
Service Company Treasurer

"This guidebook is a wonderful resource for healing. It builds self-esteem and inspires hope."

Alvin F. Poussaint, M.D.
Clinical Professor of Psychiatry, Harvard Medical School

"*Thriving At Work* is a beautiful book! Authors NB and CK have put into words the difficult emotional challenges faced every day at work by survivors of abuse. They have also provided specific tools and guidelines for creating safety at work, taking care of oneself, and developing effective coping strategies and professional behaviors. The suggestions are so gentle and kind that the reader can begin to believe in the possibility of humanizing the workplace for everyone.

While the book is intended for survivors and those who treat survivors during recovery, the contents will guide any manager and all individuals who strive to create a workplace that welcomes the sacred. I found myself doing the exercises and delighting in the possibility of making positive changes in my work environment and professional relationships. The authors describe the quality of thriving in one's own work. In all of my reading on career development and career satisfaction, I have never seen this better said. This work is inspired."

Kit Harrington Hayes, M.Ed.
Former Director of Adult and Alumni/ae Career Services,
Northeastern University
Author of *Managing Career Transitions: Your Career As A Work In Progress*

"I use the book daily in my work. When I first meet with victims I give them a copy of page 16, a list of common difficulties survivors of trauma are especially likely to face, and see which items they can identify for themselves. This starts a dialogue and an awareness and education process. I use the book to break the cycle of abuse."

Carol Mangiacotti, B.A.
Safe Plan Advocate, Massachusetts Office of Victim
Assistance

"As a career guidance publication, the *National Business Employment Weekly* receives hundreds of new books on job hunting and career strategies each year... I decided to go through the stacks and mention a few of the more compelling offerings. *Thriving At Work: A Guidebook for Survivors of Childhood Abuse*... was unique and thought-provoking enough to recommend.

Thriving At Work is the first book I've seen that explores the relationship between childhood abuse and job or career choices. Created as a workbook, the guide is designed to help employees identify and overcome workplace issues caused by their earlier trauma."

Perri Capell, Former Editor
Wall Street Journal, National Business Employment Weekly

What people are saying...

"I have really enjoyed using *Thriving At Work* with my clients. It is very easy to read and provides a variety of practical and effective methods to help a person succeed. I find that even my most limited client is able to follow the workbook. I have been recommending it to some of my colleagues who have also found it to be beneficial in working with their clients. I thank you for putting together a comprehensive and user friendly guide to succeed in both business and life."

Miguel Angel Medina, LICSW
Clinical Coordinator, Morris Heights Health Center
Psychotherapist in Private Practice, New York City

"A must read for mental health professionals. *Thriving At Work* provides thoughtful and useful counsel and exercises for anyone looking for a job or seeking to thrive in the workplace. The authors provide a template that will be useful for individual clients, as well as a structured format for group leaders to facilitate."

Susan Berger, Ed.D.
Licensed Psychologist

"*Thriving At Work: A Guidebook for Survivors of Childhood Abuse* speaks with wisdom and confidence about the challenges posed by work environments for those with histories of abuse. It does not understate the hurdles or the myriad ways that the work world can replicate childhood experiences of hierarchical relationships and abuse of power. Yet the book offers a wealth of practical guidance and inspirational language to communicate the message that an abusive childhood does not have to mean the loss of professional or financial or creative potential. I recommend this book to all adult survivors and their therapists."

Janina Fisher, Ph.D.
Past President, New England Society for the Treatment of Trauma and Dissociation

Instructor and Senior Supervisor, The Trauma Center

Executive Council, International Society for Trauma and Dissociation

EMDR International Association Approved Consultant and Credit Provider

"*Thriving At Work* is an excellent resource for any manager or supervisor. As a business owner, I now have a better understanding of the ramifications associated with a trauma background. One of my staff exhibits extreme reactions to commonplace issues, admits she feels like a fraud, and has an acute aversion to change, which are just a few of the common issues listed in your book as patterns experienced by abuse survivors. With this new awareness, we have been able to address some of her fears and self doubt, and begin to increase her effectiveness on the job."

Dee Balliett, M.S. in Mental Health Counseling
Chief of Operations, NAPFA Registered Fee-Only Financial Advisor, Balliett Financial Services, Inc.

Officer, National Association of Personal Financial Advisors South Region

Co-author of *Resource Planning: The Internet, Money & You; Your Financial Plan is a Vision of Riches; Your Financial Plan*

What people are saying...

"Thriving At Work provides inspiration and hope to people who have given up on how to make positive changes in their work situation. The clear, concise and supportive exercises provide an easy step-by-step process that empowers my clients to action. The insightful questions (such as Exercise 8, Criteria for a Healthy Work Environment) helps people question what is and envision what they deserve. A powerful and much needed book!"

Gail Liebhaber, M.Ed.
Principal, Career Directions

"Thriving at Work is an important resource for psychotherapists assisting clients with work related decisions. The book illustrates in an easy to understand format, the connection between one's trauma history and its impact in the workplace. It provides valuable tools to help make good decisions about one's job choices and work environment. In addition, there are effective strategies and tools to take care of oneself at work that have helped clients feel safer and more in control, resulting in an improved work experience."

Pat Bruno, LICSW
Psychotherapist/Career Counselor

"Finally, there is a tool to give hope to those struggling with post traumatic stress. *Thriving At Work* clearly illuminates the pitfalls that so many survivors experience as a result of past trauma. The book provides invaluable down-to-earth explanations plus lists of options and exercises. Each reader is given a roadmap pointing out blocks to success, alternatives to help deal with self-doubt, unexpected situations and difficult people, and methods to enhance personal effectiveness. Many of the strategies and exercises listed in the book have become an important part of our curriculum in helping homeless veterans achieve their employment goals."

Debby Wiesen, M.B.A., M.L.S.
Director of Training and Employment, New England Shelter for Homeless Veterans

"An exceptional book, well written and a must read for both survivors and employers. It provides a realistic approach and teaches grounded techniques to help survivors deal with every day issues. It should be a staple for every human resource department."

Gary Bergeron, Executive Director
The T.R.U.S.T. Foundation
Author of *Don't Call Me a Victim: Faith, Hope & Sexual Abuse in the Catholic Church*

2014

To My Dearest Sis,

You are such a bright light and beacon of loving wisdom and compassion whose "presence" illuminates the possibilities available. Always looking forward and showing us all how to thrive. You are a treasured gift!!!

Love always,

Cynth Kirchin

A GUIDEBOOK
FOR
SURVIVORS OF
CHILDHOOD ABUSE

THRIVING
AT
WORK

NANCY BROOK
CYNTHIA KRAININ

Thriving At Work: A Guidebook for Survivors of Childhood Abuse

Published in the United States

Career Resources, Book Department
1674 Beacon Street, Brookline, MA 02445

Second Printing 2006

To order book contact: career_resources@verizon.net or (617) 732-1200

Library of Congress Control Number 2004103296

Brook, Nancy; Krainin, Cynthia

Thriving At Work: A Guidebook for Survivors of Childhood Abuse

Includes bibliographical references.

ISBN 0966476603

1. Self Help - Psychology, overcoming effects of childhood abuse at work. 2. Recovery. 3. Careers - Business - Reference. 4. Health, Mind & Body.

Cover Design: Josh Meyer, Cambridge, MA
Printer: King Printing, Lowell, MA
Logo: Linda Michaels, Boston, MA

DEDICATION

Our book is dedicated to all survivors of childhood abuse – be it physical, sexual, or emotional – who take on each day of their lives with resilience, strength of spirit, and courage, and who know that despite whatever terror may reside within, they will get through this day.

We thank all who have shared with us their experiences and lives as survivors – in individual counseling sessions and in our workshops. Your perspective has taught us how to help, and has allowed us to be partners in your healing and your thriving.

Thriving At Work was written in 1998. Several years later, the dark secret about clergy abuse of children came to light. We want to acknowledge the male and female survivors of clergy abuse whose courage to step forward and tell their stories provide the spotlight necessary to expose perpetrators and demonstrate the legacy of childhood abuse.

To those who keep their own counsel about this horrific trauma, we want to tell you that you are not forgotten in your silence.

STATISTICS ON CHILD ABUSE:
THE HARD FACTS

Did You Know That...

♦ There are over 60 million adult survivors of childhood abuse.

♦ It is estimated that 1 in every 5 adults who live in the U.S. is a child abuse survivor.

♦ More than 2.9 million reports of abuse or neglect concerning 5.5 million children were received by child protective services agencies in 2003.

♦ The actual incidence of abuse and neglect is estimated to be 3 times greater than the number reported to authorities.

♦ Child abuse is reported - on average - every 10 seconds.

♦ In 2003, it was reported that 48% of abuse victims were male; 52% were female.

♦ 70 cases a week of child abuse allegations against American churches come to the attention of the Christian Ministry Resources.

(Statistics from 2003 National Clearinghouse Reports)

FOREWORD

By Ellen Bass

I was especially happy to find out about this book. *Thriving At Work* bridges past trauma, recovery and current work experiences. It is sensible, insightful and gives good concrete suggestions and advice. The authors are concise – a special accomplishment.

For survivors of abuse, the workplace becomes a dramatic backdrop where past childhood painful feelings are played out. Old wounds may become exacerbated, leaving an employee feeling vulnerable and unsafe. Without learning about and understanding how past hurts show up on the job, work can eventually become unbearable.

Thriving At Work educates and offers new coping skills for managing re-stimulating experiences. There are many valuable books on healing from abuse; however, very few are solely devoted to the job. This is so important.

This book is invaluable to counselors, the human resource community, the larger community and to those whose biggest wish is to leave the past behind and become whole and thrive.

> Ellen Bass is co-author of *The Courage to Heal: A Guide for Women Survivors of Child Sexual Abuse* (Ellen Bass and Laura Davis) 1994, HarperPerennial Library. Ellen is a recipient of numerous national literacy awards for poetry. Most notable is her work: *Mules of Love: Poems, American Poets Continuum,* 2002, BOA Editions. She currently resides in California.

ACKNOWLEDGMENTS

In writing this book, we have been blessed by people who believed in us and our ability to put our wisdom into print. Our choir of supporters kept reminding us how important this book would be in the lives of the readers we wanted to reach.

We are grateful to Susan Berger, Tom Campbell, Lori Grace, Steven Holt, Margot McCain, Josh Meyer, Margaret Newhouse, and Gloria Breton for their insight, feedback, and editing suggestions and the respectful way in which they offered their advice. We acknowledge our families, friends, and colleagues for their flexibility and understanding as we devoted ourselves to this book.

A heartfelt thanks to two special people, Linda Michaels and Thayer McCain, who have stood by us and reassured us, particularly when we were balancing this project with unexpected family medical problems.

We feel fortunate to experience our work as "life work." We have been given the opportunity to use our careers as vehicles for transforming life experiences. It is gratifying to be able to express the talents we possess in ways that contribute to healing and to breaking the cyclical patterns of abuse.

CONTENTS

A Note To Our Readers

We take seriously all of the responses received from our readers. The stories of how people creatively share exercises in this book with colleagues or friends, are inspiring.

This book has found itself as the centerpiece for support groups and in corporate conference rooms where employees come together to complete exercises and discuss chapters.

One suggestion we heard frequently was the need for more writing space. In response to this comment, we are providing more space for writing in the second reprint.

Please continue to send us your stories and comments.

INTRODUCTION

The Purpose in Writing This Book

Our purpose is clear: we want you to gain control of your life by improving the quality of the minutes and hours of each workday. We offer you a blueprint for managing life at work.

It is hard to find resources and information to help those recovering from the wounds of childhood trauma. Absent are resources that enrich and empower survivors' lives and help them navigate the challenges they face at work. For years, our clients and workshop participants have asked us, "When are you going to write a book incorporating all of the tools and techniques you have developed to help me feel more in control and better able to manage my work?"

We have written this book to respond to that need. It is offered as a guide and as a resource. It provides tools, techniques, and strategies we have developed and collected over the years as career and work issues counselors. We realize the importance of extending these resources to those beyond our client base.

Everyone experiences personal challenges at work. Those with trauma backgrounds tend to react to these issues in the extreme. Here are some common difficulties survivors of trauma are especially likely to face.

- the "I am a fraud" syndrome
- under- or over-achieving
- repeatedly choosing and tolerating unhealthy, abusive job situations
- acting out at jobs
- distrust of people
- feeling victimized at work
- extreme startle response
- self-sabotaging behavior
- feeling an overall sense of powerlessness
- feeling intimidated by authority figures
- choosing extreme environments: cold and rigid or cozy and inappropriate
- being over-responsible
- being a "professional" pleaser or fixer
- perfectionism
- feeling invisible and unheard

- spotty/scattered job history
- procrastination
- history of personality conflicts
- depression
- addictions
- needing to be in control
- alienation and isolation
- obsessive relationships at work
- immune deficiency illnesses
- being highly critical of self and others
- overwhelming feelings of fear and anxiety
- compulsive behavior or workaholism
- blaming self for others' moods
- avoiding direct communication
- feelings of shame
- lack of meaning in work and life
- negating accomplishments as flukes
- accepting of all behaviors

Our Audience

First and foremost, our book is for the adult who has experienced childhood trauma and is trying to make sense of the past and understand how it impacts the present. It is for adults who experienced significant neglect as children and/or were deprived of the social structures that foster the development of a healthy self-image. You may be someone who knows or supports a person who has old wounds to heal. This book links the legacy of childhood abuse to jobs, careers, and livelihood.

Today, in too many families there is significant physical, emotional and/or sexual abuse, alcoholism and substance abuse. Parents are unable to provide nurturance and guidance to foster the sense of self each child requires. In addition to the home, abuse occurs in school settings, churches, athletic programs, camps, spiritual communities, etc.

Who is a survivor?

We talk about survivors who as children had to shut down, repress, and deny events and feelings unfolding in their young lives. The world they lived in was unsafe and threatening. They are survivors because despite the deep wounding that occurred, they have persevered, relying on their intrinsic spirit to survive.

The ramifications of past trauma are significant. Though every person's history is different, each survivor is holding a wounded child within. That makes the adult survivor more vulnerable and prone to respond to life's challenges from the perspective of a hurt child. The legacy of abuse usually produces an adult with low self-esteem, a poor self-image, and therefore, a reduced capacity to function as an effective adult.

Childhood abuse, like many toxins, alters everything in life. Children are deeply affected by outbursts of rage and/or continuing depression from a parent who may be struggling with substance abuse and job instability due to their own past wounds. This has a ripple effect. Without help or intervention, abused adults who become parents, traumatize their children, repeating the toxic pattern.

Child abuse impacts the individual and society. Personal creativity, accomplishment, and ability to make a contribution to the whole are stymied leaving at least 20% of the population unable to lead full, satisfying lives.

Do you struggle with long-term low self-esteem and question your self-worth?

You might not consider yourself a "survivor." Yet, if you experience long-term low self-esteem and question your self-worth, you may relate to many of the challenges we address in this book.

It would be impossible to create a list of people who help survivors on a daily basis. We have identified a sampling of professionals in local communities who can utilize this book to provide care and understanding to a survivor.

Put this book in the hands of:

therapists	clergy
work colleagues	friends
work supervisors	families
trauma survivors	sponsors
health care centers	nutritionists
community centers	body workers
health care providers	support groups
correctional institutions	fitness specialists
educators at every level	recovery programs
managers and supervisors	physical therapists
human resource specialists	life and work coaches
employee assistance programs	occupational therapists
treatment and rehabilitation centers	juvenile detention centers

Our Philosophy

Ultimately, people want to have control over their work and the choices they make in their job life. We feel this is best accomplished by acquiring knowledge and by being prepared. We want to inspire you to take control of your worklife and to know that you can directly influence your experience at work.

Throughout this book we highlight the phrase, "I will create a healthy working environment by shifting my perspective and expectations through knowledge and self-effort." We repeat this phrase to reinforce and validate that you already have what you need to thrive. It is strategically placed to remind you that although there are specific issues related to being a survivor, it does not mean you are "flawed," have a personality defect or are eccentric by nature.

Repeating the phrase affirms that change can come through awareness, education, and effort to affect the course of your life. The strengths you have developed and used to get you to this point can be harnessed and linked with new knowledge, self-effort, and faith to create the kind of worklife you deserve.

> *You may have been told or have felt that you are "flawed," have a personality defect or are eccentric by nature. This is usually not the case.*

> *Many times what you are experiencing is the cause and effect of past traumatic moments in your life.*

How To Use This Book

Designed to help you thrive during your workday, we organize our material in an easy-to-use menu format that will facilitate personal choices and support you in honoring your own individual process.

Thriving At Work is intended to give you a road map with plenty of options for you to use at your own pace. We do not suggest a specific timeline for integrating the contents of this book.

> ***Remember to be kind to yourself. Be compassionate with yourself. Honor the timing of your own process.***

You will find this publication written in a practical, hands-on style. The chapter topics we have selected are the foundation pieces necessary for designing and building a thriving work container and climate. We believe that with these pieces in place, you can step out with confidence into the world, expressing fully your innate talents and gifts.

Chapter 1 explores the work stressors and coping mechanisms survivors rely on to manage stress. In this chapter, we also describe how a strong work or vocational identity is formed.

Chapters 2 and 3 focus on how to create safety and how to nurture yourself. These chapters lay the foundation to enable you to achieve competency in all aspects of the workplace.

Chapter 4 is devoted to difficult situations that can paralyze a survivor at work. Empowering responses to difficult work scenarios are offered to teach new skills and assertive behavior.

In Chapter 5 you will be reminded of the common strengths and attributes that you possess as a survivor. Abuse survivors, not surprisingly, underestimate and underutilize their strengths.

In Chapter 6 we introduce both the expected stages of the healing process and the job choices that correspond to these stages. The healing stages that we suggest in this book are useful in matching functional capabilities with corresponding jobs. Please keep in mind that they do not necessarily reflect each individual's process.

Chapter 7 helps you clarify and define your personal criteria for a healthy work environment. Knowing what to look for in a work setting and assessing the environment before taking a job will increase the potential for a longer and more positive job experience.

Chapter 8 captures how you can move from surviving to thriving in the workplace. It will provide rich material for understanding the qualities a thriver brings to the workplace.

Chapter 9 offers ways to continue the integration of what you found most important in this book. Included are very specific suggestions that can become personal strategies and be incorporated into your every day worklife.

The exercises and inventories listed in the back of the book will reference you to the writing sections of this book. These exercises are designed to facilitate a shift from struggling and surviving to thriving and flourishing at work. At times, you may find these exercises to be grounding and you can use them as a stepping stone towards action, while at other times they may stimulate thinking and/or awareness.

Thriving At Work: A Guidebook For Survivors of Childhood Abuse will be a companion in the search to understand your relationship to work. We hope that it will provide direction, motivation, support, and inspiration to guide you on your road to a fulfilling worklife.

CHAPTER ONE

Work, Stress, and Vocational Identity

The workplace of today challenges everyone's ability to manage stress while staying focused on developing or maintaining a strong work identity. Demands on workers today are excessive because of reduced resources, downsizing, and the ever-increasing challenges of balancing work, personal life, and family life.

Trauma survivors not only face the challenges of the twenty-first century, but also grapple with trying to understand the impact of childhood neglect and abuse on work and career choices.

Those with trauma backgrounds are often not familiar with the idea of flourishing at work. Abuse survivors are too busy managing internal feelings and trying to stay safe to be concerned with thriving. What would it be like to thrive and have a balanced life rather than be driven by stress and fear?

Understanding And Managing The Stressors

Stress is part of everyday living. Some stress is normal, and a certain level of stress is actually a good thing. Successfully managing all the types of stress we encounter takes commitment and practice. Through education, awareness, and insight, you can begin to have different responses to the various stressors and feel more in control of your life at work.

A type of stress specific to the workplace is occupational stress which is associated with situations where employees feel a lack of control and autonomy. This book addresses how this stress is experienced by trauma survivors.

"Work is not safe. The world is not safe. I am not safe. I am powerless." When this is your belief system, it is no wonder the workplace drains your life energy. Just making it through the workday may require hypervigilance, self-protection, coping and numbing out in order to survive.

Workplace as a "War Zone"

Navigating land mines	Terrified
A deer caught in headlights	Trapped
Fear of not getting out alive	Powerless
The wolf is just around the corner	Unprotected

Survivors frequently use these expressions to describe life at work. These are terrifying images – usually associated with the experience of war. It is not surprising then, that some trauma survivors also cope with post-traumatic stress disorder – the diagnosis veterans of war have been treated for since 1920.

If you are someone who is: grateful just for making it through the day without being hurt or shamed, your attention and energy cannot be directed. Protecting yourself on a daily basis keeps you from expressing your creativity, fulfilling goals, and realizing the moments of success and achievement that make up a good day at work. Your career is impeded by the legacy of old, unresolved terrors and hurts.

The work environment can easily become a stage where family abuse and trauma events are reenacted. In the workplace, a power differential always exists with authority figures. Co-workers may resemble siblings competing for approval from the authority figure. Work expectations elicit old fears of making mistakes and paying for them later. Long hours in the same setting contribute to feeling trapped. It takes very little to have old responses "triggered" and then to react to a work situation in the same way one would have coped in the family.

Many psycho-spiritual books tell us that situations in life repeatedly give us opportunities for continued healing and growth. It is fascinating to notice that the people with whom we have the most conflict in the workplace have personalities and behaviors similar to those in our lives with whom we need to do more healing. And when these issues are resolved, many times the intensity of these personalities and their impact diminishes.

I feel like a fraud

Why is it that abuse survivors feel flawed, believing that acquiring good jobs is just a fluke? We must realize that abuse actually changes the structure of the brain. It is no surprise that negating the Self is common among survivors.

It is easy to understand why abuse survivors relive trauma at work and have difficulty separating the past from the present. This is complicated by the way organizations have historically managed employees. Too many organizations are still fear-driven, competitive, and authoritarian, fostering management styles that disempower their human capital.

More is being written in business publications about team-building and motivating workers in a more respectful, collaborative, and value-based style. Companies are beginning to respond to this wave of change by paying more attention to and investing in their internal community.

Learned Coping Styles For Dealing With Stress

Authors Ellen Bass and Laura Davis are well known for identifying the issues and challenges facing survivors of sexual abuse. In *The Courage To Heal Workbook,* Laura Davis describes the range of coping patterns survivors rely on to deal with stress in their lives. Some coping mechanisms she identifies are:

- perfectionism
- spacing out
- repeating abuse
- insomnia/excessive sleeping

- forgetting
- minimizing
- creating chaos
- compulsive eating

- addictions
- staying busy
- running away
- avoiding intimacy

Although these behaviors may once have been life-saving because they effectively managed high-stress situations, relying on them takes an enormous toll on the body, psyche, and spirit over the years. Creativity is diminished and social skills are underdeveloped. These patterns distract one from being present in life.

It is easy to hold onto coping mechanisms that no longer serve you.

Some coping mechanisms become a way of being in the world. You can be so attached to a coping style that even when you know there is another option, you revert to an old behavior automatically.

**Do you relate to any of these behaviors
that hinder job success and achievement?**

Workaholism; dissociation; lack of focus; feeling exploited; poor sense of work and personal boundaries; obsession with an authority figure; negating positive feedback; needing to feel special; lapses in memory; assuming blame for everything; major personality conflicts; being triggered and going numb; angry outbursts; being solicitous; acting in self-sabotaging ways; lying; taking on roles at work that replicate family patterns (lost child, caretaker, peacekeeper, rebel or scapegoat).

EXERCISE #1: *Learned Coping Styles*

When you are in a highly stressful situation at work, what coping mechanisms do you rely on to get through the stress?

Write down three coping behaviors that you automatically revert to.

1.

2.

3.

How do these coping behaviors serve you during a stressful time?

In what ways do they hinder or distract you from being present at work?

Use this space to assess the value of these behaviors in your life today.

You will need a wider menu of coping strategies to shift from struggling at work to thriving. The upcoming chapters in this book will help you develop a constellation of healthy coping mechanisms.

Seeking And Forming A Vocational Identity

We each have a natural desire to achieve, accomplish, contribute, and feel a sense of value in the work we do. Meaningful activity fosters a sense of self-fulfillment and satisfaction. The term "vocational identity" defines how a person translates self-knowledge and life experiences into a perception of themselves in relation to work and career.

Survivors of childhood abuse must shift how they see themselves in the world in preparation for the formation of a vocational identity. To what degree do you:

- See the world as a place to thrive rather than a dangerous, unsafe territory.

- Investigate interests, authentic competencies, and abilities; believing you have preferences and choices.

- Build a strong sense of self: healing from shame, finding resources and supports that will help strengthen your inner belief in self and a future.

- Strive for positive life and work experiences to reinforce a desire to achieve. Use these experiences to begin crafting a career path.

Vocational theory suggests that successful vocational identity is determined by three competency areas:

- Knowing who you are: having an accurate and well-defined knowledge of interests, competencies, abilities, and preferences.

- Self-confidence: a belief that you have talents; belief in your ability to determine a future using available resources and personal skills.

- Positive life or work experiences to draw on and move from in determining a career path.

People generally develop these three competency areas over a life span, beginning in early childhood. Those with trauma backgrounds find themselves with insufficient development in the significant growth points in life.

It is reassuring to know that there are *specific* reasons why job-related experiences have been painful or problematic. It can be a relief to know that it is not because of a personality flaw or because you are broken and need to be fixed. A common characteristic of survivors of childhood trauma is the belief that the problems of life are rooted in a deep personality defect.

> *Remember, many of the issues survivors face*
> *are directly linked to early trauma.*

Although abuse survivors aspire towards a well formed work-identity, realizing a vocational identity may seem beyond comprehension. Do not be surprised if you have a hard time relating to some of these concepts at first. But don't despair. We are proof, as are many, many others, that you **can** begin to create a strong and positive vocational identity.

The term "developmentally delayed" has often been applied to those who lacked positive reinforcement, guidance, and nurturing in identifying the interests and building the competencies that translate into a work identity.

John Bradshaw is a nationally known public speaker and author of numerous books on recovery and healing. In one of his most popular and admired books, *Homecoming: Reclaiming and Championing Your Inner Child,* he identifies stages of child development in relation to ego-strength development. The gift in his book is learning that as an adult committed to healing, these strengths can be rebuilt and strengthened by revisiting these pivotal times in life and healing the wounds and neglect associated with a particular developmental stage.

The successful mastery of competencies and self-knowledge continues and expands in early adulthood. Abuse survivors find themselves stuck and unable to move effortlessly through adulthood. Knowledge about the stages of early adult development and your own particular barriers, obstacles, or unresolved blocks enhances compassion for yourself and your struggles to achieve in work.

Managing Career Transitions, written by career counselor Kit Hayes, contains adult development theory and the expected stages of career development. This book can help you assess where to put effort as you form a career identity.

Vocational identity is strengthened by continuing the self-discovery process. As a career seeker with a history of trauma, it will be necessary to address different issues in pursuit of a well-tuned work identity:

- You will need to know how to manage feelings while at work and determine what thwarts your efforts for improvement.

- Self-inquiry will be required into how you conduct relationships at work.

- You will learn and build on your mastery skills.

- You will need to feel safe enough to be proactive in directing the course of your job and career.

As you walk through the next chapters of this book, you will begin to identify and integrate the elements that will enhance your ability to manage in the workplace and establish yourself as a thriver.

> I will create a healthy working environment by shifting my perspective and expectations through knowledge and self-effort.

CHAPTER 2

Finding Safety In The Workplace

"Walking into the workplace, I find myself tightening up, anticipating what feels like preparation for battle – a battleground where there is no safe place to hide."

This experience of the workplace is shared by many who have a history of childhood trauma. The feelings of working in a "war zone" come from an inner reaction to the perception of an unsafe environment.

> *A workplace example: Your boss seems irritated and upset. You immediately believe you did something wrong. Your body goes into "fight / flight" readiness. You become terrified, anticipating a violent reaction. You begin to feel as you did when you were a child – little and scared.*

The experiences of immediate fear or terror resemble past traumas and trigger a response associated to an early traumatic event. In this moment, it is very difficult to differentiate the past from the present. You need to rely on strategies that give you a feeling of safety so that you can respond appropriately to the current situation.

Survivors of childhood abuse must devise healthy coping strategies and create a safe world for themselves before they can be present enough in the workplace to respond to its many challenges. Feeling safe must come first!

How can you feel safe in your body at work?

How can you make the environment safe, supportive, and conducive to doing your best work?

The answers are found in two distinct places:

1. Focusing on creating a place inside yourself where you feel protected and safe.
2. Adapting your physical environment.

In this book we refer to these areas as the *internal landscape* and *external landscape*.

The Internal Landscape

Feeling safe inside ourselves when it isn't safe outside

The internal landscape is essentially our inner experience – what goes on in our mind, our reactions to events, and our feelings. We all have clues for knowing the current state of our inner landscape.

SHIFTING INTERNAL CLUES

TURMOIL	PEACEFULNESS
fearfulness	confidence
hypervigilance	inner calm
panic	relaxed
anxiety	presence in the moment

We are providing exercises and techniques to shift the internal landscape from turmoil to peacefulness: a safe internal zone, a protective bubble that provides a buffer, and affirmations that bring you back to inner equilibrium.

Look for opportunities at work to take time and practice exercises #2 and #3.

EXERCISE #2: A Safe Zone

Take ten quiet minutes at home to visualize a place – imagined or real – where you can go to be completely safe. Include all the details like objects, colors, smells, and anything else you need to make it a safe place to be. Let it be a place where you can let your guard down and rest.

Once you have an image in your mind's eye, spend some time there. Then think of a password that represents this place for you. Maybe that word will be "waterfall" or "mountain top" or "ocean." Once that is established, practice using the password to transport yourself to this inner sanctuary so that when you are at work, you can bring yourself into your own safe and peaceful zone, no matter what is going on around you.

Place something in your workspace to touch and gaze at that represents your inner safe zone and reminds you that you do indeed have a special, safe place to go to at any time.

EXERCISE #3: *The Protective Bubble*

Imagine that you have a cozy invisible bubble that surrounds and protects you. You bump into its inside wall as you find yourself drifting toward what is happening around you — the outside drama.

Your task is to stay within the bubble, noticing when outside stimulation bumps into the edges of your bubble but does not affect you. Know that nothing can puncture your bubble.

Use your attention and awareness to remind yourself that you are still within the protective boundaries of the bubble. As soon as you forget you have a bubble, close your eyes and recreate it.

You have the ability to control your inner landscape. You will be surprised at how much both of these exercises will help give you a sense of safety and moments of peace.

> I will create a healthy working environment by shifting my perspective and expectations through knowledge and self-effort.

THE USE OF AFFIRMATIONS

Affirmations are short messages that state a positive sense of being. You can repeat them out loud or say them silently to yourself. Some people use affirmations successfully as a way to feel peaceful inside. The more times you repeat an affirmation to yourself each day, the stronger the effect.

Some examples of affirmations:

- *I am successfully using my grounding and boundary techniques to feel safe and in control of each workday.*
- *I have a voice in my workplace.*
- *I honor myself in everything I do.*
- *I am more than my feelings.*
- *This soon will pass.*
- *I am creating things that are even better than I imagined them to be.*
- *I feel safe and productive knowing I have techniques to assist me as the day progresses.*
- *I am safe right now.*
- *Anger is not violence.*
- *My energy is calm, focused, and directed toward my immediate goal.*

External Landscape

Adapting the work environment to feel safe and secure

The external landscape is everything outside us that stimulates a response, both positively and negatively. If we pay attention, we have clues available to us about our responses *TO* the external landscape that enable us to take corrective action.

SHIFTING EXTERNAL CLUES

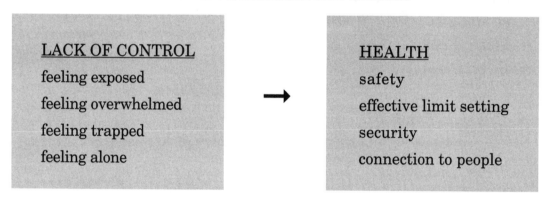

LACK OF CONTROL

feeling exposed

feeling overwhelmed

feeling trapped

feeling alone

→

HEALTH

safety

effective limit setting

security

connection to people

Five inventories are developed on the following pages to guide you in making the personal changes you want in the external landscape.

INVENTORY #1: *Physical Safety*

How can you modify your work situation to avoid surprise noises, unexpected interruptions, or feeling trapped?

- ❑ *Move your desk or chair; create a visible "aisle" that people pass through to find you.*

- ❑ *Create routine by selecting a standard location to meet a crew, colleagues or vendors.*

- ❑ *Utilize neutral open spaces to conduct your work.*

- ❑ *Place a framed photo in a position that allows you to see behind you.*

- ❑ *Put up a barrier – a file cabinet with a plant on top, or a divider that doubles as a bulletin board and a place to post notes.*

- ❑ *Use your car or truck as a safe haven; keep comforting items around.*

- ❑ *Arrange your work station in front of a window, creating a psychological way out.*

- ❑ *Place a dish of candy on your desk to provide a buffer as people approach you.*

- ❑ *Wear clothes to work that protect and comfort you. Layers of clothes can create a feeling of comfort and safety; pockets enable you to carry soothing objects. Don't wear clothes that make you feel vulnerable.*

- ❑ *Buy a "Computer Mirrored Ball" at an office supply store and place it on top of your monitor to notice movement in the room.*

Physical Safety (continued)

❑ *Other options:*

From the menu above, pick options you will commit to.

INVENTORY #2: *Personal Ground Rules*

Tell yourself:

❏ *"I have the right to feel safe at work."*

❏ *"I have the right to be respected at work."*

❏ *"When I am feeling harassed, degraded, etc., I will leave the area immediately or create a protective bubble around me."*

❏ *"I can say no to anyone at work, no matter what they ask of me."*

❏ *"No one has the right to hurt me verbally, emotionally, or physically in the workplace."*

❏ *"If I get scared, it's all right to call my therapist, a supportive friend, my sponsor, or someone whom I've identified as a safe person at work."*

❏ *"I can be clear and express my needs to my boss and co-workers."*

❏ *"I will stop and breathe deeply three times when I feel off balance."*

❏ *Other options:*

From the menu above, pick options you will commit to.

INVENTORY #3: A Work Container With Boundaries

❑ *Remind yourself that you have the right to create communication rules with good boundaries.*

❑ *Use e-mail – a less intimate style of communication – to conduct business.*

❑ *Think of how you would like people to give you messages and how you prefer to be interrupted.*

❑ *Consider leaving specific times on your voicemail when you will return calls (to buy yourself time and space).*

❑ *Schedule meetings at your convenience as often as possible.*

❑ *Establish your desk and files as yours, and not for others to look through or touch without asking.*

❑ *Think of and suggest a good time and way to discuss an important topic.*

❑ *Observe how peers have established rules for themselves and communicated them to others.*

❑ *Put a note on your door about knocking and about interrupting. Establish a signal that lets other staff know that you do not want to be interrupted. When your door is closed, or when you are using an unused office or conference room, post a sign indicating that you do not want to be disturbed.*

❑ *Arrange alternative times to discuss business with someone to avoid feeling put on the spot. (See "Handling Hard Situations on the Job," Chapter 4, page 65)*

❑ *Remind yourself that work will generally take place between 9 and 5.*

❑ *Take a lunch break each day AND take two paid 15 minute breaks each day (as allowed by law).*

❑ *Other options:*

From the menu above, pick options you will commit to.

INVENTORY #4: A Safe, Protective Space

❑ *Choose people who are nurturing and keep a list of their names, e-mail addresses, or telephone numbers handy.*

❑ *Place a special picture or saying on your wall or in your car.*

❑ *Make your own work space calm. Use pictures, a trophy, a cushion, a stone, a desk aquarium, or objects that remind you of calm places. Make a list of things you find calming to refer to.*

❑ *Stop for a cup of tea before you return to the home office to meet with the boss.*

❑ *Personalize a tool to remind you every time you use it that you are in control (a tool can be: a hammer, a PDA, cell phone, stapler, iPod, wallet or change container in your car).*

❑ *Look for a place at work where you can retreat if necessary, like a conference room, bathroom, a parking lot, empty closet, or basement.*

❑ *Occasionally visit your worksite over the weekend to clean up and prepare for the coming week.*

❑ *Do something soothing before you begin your day.*

❑ *If you have a meditation practice, remember that you can meditate for even one or two minutes during the day to center yourself. You can arrive ten minutes early to work and begin your day with a meditation. If possible, have calm background music on hand, an affirmation, or a mantra to say during the day to calm and restore yourself.*

❑ *If you like nature, identify an outdoor area that you pass on your way to work that you find calming. Plan to stop there for at least 5 minutes each day.*

❑ *Find a window in your office building that has a nice view. Make short visits there during the day.*

❑ *Write down ways that you created safety in your work environment.*

❑ *Other options:*

From the menu above, pick options you will commit to.

INVENTORY #5: A Supportive Network

In building a support network, can you identify people who are:

❑ *Validating*

❑ *Stable*

❑ *Good listeners*

❑ *Empathetic*

❑ *Calm*

❑ *Mature*

❑ *Humorous*

❑ *Approachable*

❑ *Able to keep confidentiality*

❑ *Caring*

❑ *Non-judgmental*

❑ *Able to give a reality check*

❑ *Capable of giving feedback in a constructive and helpful way*

❑ *Able to acknowledge you and your strengths*

❑ *Inspiring*

A Supportive Network (continued)

❏ *Creative thinkers*

❏ *Hopeful*

❏ *Able to see the big picture*

❏ *Encouraging*

❏ *Self-assured*

❏ *Mentor oriented*

❏ *Respected by others*

❏ *Self-forgiving*

❏ *Seen as achievers*

❏ *Goal-oriented*

❏ *Centered*

❏ *Directed*

❏ *Purposeful*

❏ *Other qualities:*

What are the qualities you want in people who are in your support network?

Who comes to mind when you think of the above qualities?

Identify specific characteristics that would feel supportive to you.

How do you plan to approach someone? (invite them to lunch, ask for a time to chat, call them outside of work)

What will let you know, through the conversation, that this is a potential support person for you?

Remember: reevaluate your network to ensure that it meets your current needs. Your needs will continually change. Be willing to commit to building these relationships.

Divulging at Work

How much do I tell and with whom do I share in the workplace? Abuse survivors will pose this question to themselves at different times during their worklife. There is no definitive rule that can guide you in deciding how much of your personal life is appropriate to share with people at work. Survivors benefit a great deal by sharing their stories. Breaking out of isolation and talking with others helps to build connection and to feel validated. You need to ask yourself, "What part of my life is appropriate to bring to work?"

It is easy to feel an urge to share the details of your personal life at work. It is often in retrospect that survivors have seriously questioned the value in having divulged the intimate details of their life with co-workers. The question to consider is, "Where is it appropriate and safe to share personal issues, and what are the risks?" There certainly are risks in choosing to look for support and validation at work. Use the following list to consider this question.

Potential Advantages

- Feeling understood and seen.
- Being truthful and forthright.
- Legitimizing requests for special accommodations at work.
- Creating personal friendships at work.
- Having a reason to ask for time off without lying.
- Not having to explain why some things are bothersome.
- Having a source of immediate support when needed.

Potential Disadvantages

- Finding it difficult to maintain good personal boundaries.
- Expecting more sympathy, support, and validation than is appropriate at the workplace.
- Increased employment risks and vulnerability regarding perceptions of your ability to perform your job.
- Information may be used against you.
- Fear and stereotyping may impact relationships.

Ultimately, sharing intimate information at work stretches the workplace boundaries. You may, however, feel strongly that you need special accommodations in the workplace to successfully perform your job (e.g. a flexible schedule, a quiet place to work). If this is true, then it would be appropriate to explore with your therapist the questions of disability, employment protection, and accommodation guaranteed under the guidelines of the Americans with Disabilities Act (ADA).

Choosing Safety for Yourself: A Summary

It is now time to pause, reflect, and acknowledge that you can begin to change your internal landscape as well as external environment by choosing positive, healthy, and constructive options for yourself.

From the exercises and inventories you have completed in this chapter, use the space below to summarize your personal options for designing safe internal and external environments.

A Healthy *Internal Landscape:*

⇨

⇨

⇨

⇨

A Healthy *External Landscape:*

Physical Safety:

⇨

⇨

⇨

⇨

A Work Container with Boundaries:

⇨

⇨

⇨

⇨

Personal Ground Rules:

⇨

⇨

⇨

⇨

A Safe, Protective Space:

⇨

⇨

⇨

⇨

A Supportive Network:

⇨

⇨

Continue adding other criteria to your lists as you become more aware of your needs. Prioritize the lists and begin looking for ways to adapt the external landscape in your current job site. Consider your environment. Can changes be made to enhance your worklife?

An example: asking your boss for a workspace that isn't next to the office copy machine so that you can concentrate better.

An example: at a trade show, invite a network prospect to a quiet corner of the room to talk.

Keep evaluating your prioritized criteria with an eye to assessing your changing needs.

You have more power than you think...

Design a richer work climate. In very concrete ways you can now establish practices and actions to manage and enhance both the **Internal Landscape** and **External Landscape** at the workplace. Give yourself the gift of spending focused time with the exercises and inventories we have offered in this chapter, "Finding Safety in the Workplace."

If you like brainstorming with others, invite a friend to develop criteria along with you. You may discover that together you have even more options. You will begin to feel more protected and more equipped to move into new situations and jobs with an empowered sense of knowing how to take care of yourself.

NOTES

CHAPTER 3

Nurturing And Self-Care At Work

Taking Care of Yourself

How much do you think about taking care of yourself during your hours at work?

Taking care of children and pets is spontaneous and natural. With children especially, we as adults make sure they do not overdo, that they rest regularly; and we focus on identifying and meeting their needs. We reward them for meeting challenges and give them incentives to move through difficult tasks. It is important to learn to take care of ourselves in the same way.

Nurturing and self-care are critical to creating a healthy balanced life and need to become part of your daily routine. At first, being kind and gentle to yourself might feel awkward, forced, and uncomfortable. With a little time, you will come to treasure the respite and count on it to refill the inner reservoir that can be drained by stress at work.

It is a challenge to interrupt fast-paced, habitual patterns with new behaviors. However, to sustain a positive work environment it is crucial to create a routine that includes several self-care techniques.

An example: have a cup of calming tea at your desk to start the day and repeat a positive affirmation while sipping your drink.

Beyond a routine that is balanced with self-care, there are times when allowing treats as incentives and rewards can make difficult tasks possible while at the same time nourishing the spirit and body.

An example: plan lunch with a supportive friend to follow a meeting where you spoke up directly to your boss.

Times when we **need**, but often do not give ourselves treats:

- following a difficult decision

- prior to standing up for yourself

- following a flashback or panic attack

- upon completion of a task or part of a project

As a way to inspire yourself to create your own repertoire of treats, incentives, and self-care habits, take a few moments to complete the following exercise.

EXERCISE #4: *Identifying Self-Care Techniques*

List of Self-Care Techniques

- ❑ Arrange for a massage
- ❑ Browse the Internet
- ❑ Buy a treat, favorite magazine, clothing, flowers, CD, book
- ❑ Call a "fun" person
- ❑ Clean out one drawer
- ❑ Create a list of your positive attributes
- ❑ Doodle
- ❑ Eat a favorite food
- ❑ Enjoy a hot tub/sauna
- ❑ Fantasize a get-away vacation
- ❑ Garden
- ❑ Get a pedicure or facial
- ❑ Get extra child care

- ❑ Go away for a weekend
- ❑ Go to a movie
- ❑ Hike/ski/cycle
- ❑ Lighten the work load
- ❑ Listen to an inspiring or relaxing tape
- ❑ Look at a picture of a favorite person or pet
- ❑ Look at your folder of reference letters
- ❑ Make a list of people you want to spend time with
- ❑ Perform a comforting task
- ❑ Plan for a day off
- ❑ Play cards with friends
- ❑ Put on special music

- ❑ Quit stressful activities
- ❑ Rent a movie YOU want to watch
- ❑ Reorganize one file
- ❑ Sing a song to yourself
- ❑ Shoot hoops or play pool
- ❑ Sip a favorite drink
- ❑ Spend time with a pet
- ❑ Spend time with supportive people
- ❑ Take a walk or drive
- ❑ Take photographs
- ❑ Take planned and unplanned breaks
- ❑ Perform a random act of kindness

1. Check off items from the list above that make you feel good.

2. Add your own items to the list.

3. Check options that can be used as treats or incentives.

4. Of those items checked, circle the ones that can be included in your daily work routine.

5. Indicate activities to do after work that respond to a need at the workplace. Mark those separately.

6. Which of the circled items will become part of your regular self-care routine at work?

7. Which self-care activities will you do after work?

8. When you really need a pat on the back or a reward for having done something difficult, select and give to yourself the self-care techniques that will provide the kind of acknowledgment that you deserve!

Grounding Techniques

No matter how much intellectual understanding you have about your abuse issues, work can continue to be restimulating unless you practice ways to ground yourself in high-stress situations.

It is critical to your well-being to be able to recognize when a high-stress situation is causing you to lose touch with your body, mind, and emotions. The first step in addressing a retraumatizing situation is to become aware of the signs that indicate you have moved into a fragile internal state.

When a person experiences traumatic stress, the body, mind, and psyche are deeply affected. The heart races; the mind goes numb; panic sets in. There is an immediate and spontaneous urge to flee. It is hard to stay connected to the body. This reaction causes you to feel ungrounded and unfocused.

Managing high-stress situations with *immediate* grounding techniques will help to achieve the desired goal of being fully present and functioning well at work. Remember, each person is different. For some, regular breathing exercises throughout the day is enough to stay grounded and feeling centered.

Some abuse survivors talk of going to great lengths to avoid situations dealing with people because of the fear that an interaction could escalate, become terrifying and possibly dangerous. This happens because the coping mechanisms you learned to help you as a child, tend to be "default" behavior throughout your adult life.

It is crucial to establish new practices for responding in moments of traumatic stress with healthy coping mechanisms – to have a "toolbox" full of grounding techniques to draw from when anticipating a stressful interaction. If your work history resembles a "war zone" and is filled with retraumatizing events, you will naturally associate the world of work with trauma.

An example: if you were caught in a conversation with someone who started talking in a condescending or blaming way, would you freeze, dissociate, go into a panic attack, start feeling small and powerless, or become verbally abusive yourself? Or would you know to...

... breathe, breathe again; focus on something behind that person to stay present; have a prepared response that buys you time but is appropriate to the situation (see "Handling Hard Situations on the Job," Chapter 4, page 65); know how to refocus and regroup after the event so that you will not be emotionally disabled for the rest of the day.

> I will create a healthy working environment by shifting my perspective and expectations through knowledge and self-effort.

We have collected an extensive sampling of proven grounding techniques that can keep you calm and bring you back to the present moment. Some can be used in or out of the workplace and others are not appropriate within the work setting. Integrating these techniques into your daily life will greatly reduce the amount of occupational stress you experience. Practicing grounding techniques on a regular basis will help you feel in control at work.

Ultimately with this repertoire of tools and with time, your association with work as a traumatic "war zone" will fade.

INVENTORY #6: *Grounding Techniques That Can Be Practiced At Work*

- Breathe
- Call a buddy or a support person
- Change the lighting
- Close the office door
- Conduct a physical body/pulse check
- Conduct a reality check
- Count breaths
- Count to twenty
- Distract yourself by looking out a window
- Drink a glass of water
- Eat nurturing food
- Focus on a picture/item placed on desk
- Go to your car and grasp steering wheel tightly for 30 seconds, then release it
- Grab paper and write everything you're feeling and shred it

- Identify a safe place with a door. Use it as a retreat space
- Imagine putting the feeling up on a shelf; set it aside
- Imagine you are a tree sending roots deep into the earth where they are firmly planted
- Leave car or office and take a vigorous walk
- Look at a picture that represents nature
- Look at a special screen saver you put on your computer
- Loosen jaw by opening your mouth wide
- Make a cup of "grounding" tea
- Place a cool wash cloth on your forehead
- Pray/repeat a mantra
- Read a special book

- Remove yourself from the workspace and walk to a neutral area.
- Repeat an affirmation
- Remind yourself, "I have an adult self who can protect me"
- Rub a piece of clothing
- Sit with someone
- Surround yourself with a protective "bubble"
- Surround yourself with white protective light
- Take a bathroom break
- Take off shoes and plant your feet firmly on the ground
- Tell yourself, "This feeling will pass" or that you can come back to the feeling later
- Think of colors you like
- Touch an object like a ring or bracelet

Circle techniques you will commit to.

INVENTORY #7: *Grounding Techniques For Outside of Work*

- Create and practice affirmations
- Cut up paper
- Dance
- Do a short progressive muscle relaxation and visualization
- Do some physical exercise to release energy
- Do yoga stretches
- Draw a picture of your feelings

- Eat something nurturing
- Fly a kite
- Get a hug
- Get outside and walk briskly for 15-20 minutes
- Jump rope
- Light candles
- Listen to a relaxation tape
- Massage yourself
- Put on music

- Read a novel
- Scream in the car
- Shoot hoops
- Sing
- Sit in a favorite chair
- Use a punching bag
- Walk the dog
- Work in the yard
- Work on a crossword puzzle
- Write your feelings in a journal
- Yell into a pillow

❑ *Other options:*

From this menu, pick options you can commit to.

Establishing Nurturing and Self-Care Practices

Review the inventories and exercises in this chapter. Select items that you believe can be most helpful to you in taking care of yourself at work. Use the space below to summarize this information. Consider bringing these summaries with you to work.

Nurturing and Self-Care Techniques I Will Use:

Grounding Techniques I Will Use:

Establishing self-care and nurturing practices does not just happen. As with learning any new technique, it may feel awkward at first. By persevering and staying with it, it slowly gets easier.

Be especially forgiving of yourself if in one moment you forget all the healthy practices you put in place. You can begin again the next day or even the next minute! One day you will surprise yourself by spontaneously applying new techniques and handling a tough moment with much less distress.

Remember to be compassionate and tender with yourself.

At any time you can take out your book, come back to this section, and reacquaint yourself with the self-care practices you believe will work best for you. Begin again, and again, and again. Noticing, without judging, that you have strayed from your intention. This is an important part of the process of healing.

CHAPTER 4

Handling Hard Situations On The Job

In our workshops for survivors and in our individual counseling sessions with clients, we find that many people are ill-equipped to handle difficult dynamics at work. If you think about it, where did you learn to handle, with diplomacy and a sense of strength, difficult conversations or encounters?

We all admire people who possess objectivity, business savvy, and diplomacy, and who also approach others with respect, and an open mind and heart. They exhibit skills and qualities that can be acquired.

Having the skills to respond to unexpected circumstances is one way to feel in control at work. It is helpful to observe others, to learn from their successes and failures. Try some new approach to see how it feels. Try it a few times. Look for opportunities to practice new responses. It will help you to feel ready and able to respond to whatever comes your way.

A Survey: High-Stress Work Scenarios

In compiling material for this book, we designed a questionnaire listing many hard situations experienced in the workplace. We sent it to survivors of childhood abuse and asked which situations caused the most stress. The following examples represent a sampling of the most stressful situations reported by the respondents. With each example, we offer at least one possible new coping response.

As you read each high-stress work situation, write down other appropriate responses that come to mind.

1. *I feel overworked and my boss asks me to take on another project. How do I tell him no?*

   First, collect yourself. Ask, "Could we meet later today to talk about my workload? I'd like to sit down with you and look at my current projects, including the new one you have in mind, and prioritize the lot to see if and how the new project could fit in." Or ask, "Is it critical that I take this on immediately? There seems to be some priority (deadline) around the one I'm working on right now. Can we schedule a time later this morning or afternoon to talk about all of this?"

   "Right now I'm spread really thin. When I have completed tasks x, y and z, I could take on this new one. Can this wait until later, perhaps?" If the answer is no, try to arrange a time to meet when you have had time to regroup, and then explain, "My plate is full. What do you think makes sense to take off my plate in order to add this new project and set the right priority?"

• Breathe	• State the problem
• Buy time	• Think of the solution

2. *My idea is discussed at a meeting and people start cutting it down. I get overwhelmed with feelings of humiliation, stupidity, shame, etc. What do I do and say to get through this situation?*

Notice your feelings. Neutralize the situation by telling yourself that they are responding to an idea, NOT TO YOU. The idea is neutral, and you could have had similar responses to someone else's idea. Breathe, and when you add input, respond by saying, "Your comments are interesting. I'd like to consider them and resubmit this idea" or "Interesting feedback. How about if I (or we) integrate some of these ideas as we move forward?" or "I'm interested in your response. Tell me more."

The goal is to depersonalize. Be positive, not defensive. At work people are responding to products, ideas, tasks, and not to you personally. "Normalizing," or personally detaching yourself, will go a long way in helping you stay neutral in a potentially "hot" moment.

"At the moment, I'm really attached to this idea. Why don't I take your comments back to my desk, get some perspective, work on it, and send you my reworked proposal?"

"I realize that I'm emotionally attached to this idea. I should step back and get some perspective. Why don't we take a five-minute break, and then resume?"

3. *I find myself pulled into other peoples' problems at work. How do I keep from feeling weighted down by the work issues of my colleagues?*

If you are the person that co-workers always come to when they need to talk, it is important to determine how much you contribute to this dilemma. Ask yourself, "What do I get from being the person people can come to for comfort or advice?"

You use the word weighted. Are you saying you are burdened by the issues of others? If so, why do you keeping getting engaged? Is it hard to disengage with certain people? Are you worried that if you pull back you will lose something or lose this person's attention? You can still be there for another without giving them permission to "vent."

When you feel pulled toward someone and their problems, notice the feeling that is coming up for you. **Don't act on that feeling.** Just sit with it and notice. In fact, engage in something else or with someone else immediately. Practice doing this and notice what it is like for you to not be the person jumping in. You may experience more feelings when you choose not to act. Look at those feelings.

Practice keeping conversations about neutral topics. "How was your weekend?" If the answer is the beginning of complaining and problems, you can say, "I'm sorry to hear that. I hope it changes for you." Then move on to another topic. That person will eventually see you as someone they can connect with but in an alternative way. Or, the person may move on to someone else who will replace you as someone who will fill that need. In either case, you will feel relieved about the outcome and can be more present to yourself.

You may also notice loss: Loss of being in a drama, loss of an adrenalin moment, loss of giving someone your advice, loss of being important to someone in that way; loss of being needed. Loss can be part of letting go of a trait that gave you something back. Everyone once in a while has to feel that loss as part of growing personally or making different choices in life.

Note: In many workplaces, there is an individual that may seem to have a green light in front of them and/or a sign that states "Open door -- wide open heart. Bring your troubles to me." This person seems to take on a human resource role. Notice that this individual may have difficulties with boundaries, may spend less time doing productive work and more time chatting with people, or is always overly interested in the details as a way of feeling connected and needed.

4. *I am so good at taking care of others. How can I take care of myself at work?*

This behavior will begin to change when you understand what is motivating the caretaking. Once you know that it often has to do with hoping others will like you, you can get reassurance from friends that you are well-liked just by being yourself. If it feels like a compulsion you cannot control, it may be appropriate to talk with a counselor or a friend. Balance between being there for another and taking care of yourself takes constant awareness.

Consider adjusting some of your caretaking behavior. Experiment with not responding immediately to a need and see what happens. Watch the outcome. Take notes about the process and outcome. Notice your feelings.

At work people will expect what they are given. A caretaker may establish patterns at work that invite people to take advantage of the willing "giver." Eventually the pattern will lead to bitterness and resentment on the part of the caretaker. By being totally attentive to others' needs, you are not able to tune into your own. As long as you take care of someone else, you do not deal with your own fear of potential anger, of being judged, or of being rejected.

5. *I am so fearful of making a mistake that I make even more than I would normally. What can I do to control my fears of failure and of making a mistake?*

Notice the fear. Ask yourself, "What am I afraid of? Is this really likely to happen? Is this response connected to what is happening right now?" Get feedback. Call a friend or sponsor and talk it through. Ask yourself, "If I were not trying to do this perfectly, how would I approach it? If I were not in fear, how would I approach this?"

Give yourself permission to do it less than perfectly. Self-talk with affirmations: "The best I can do will be fine." Negotiate with the fear and move forward. Even a company president will make small and BIG mistakes and continue to move ahead with the work. Staying attached to perfection drains your energy and distracts you from your creativity.

Note: if you are in a new position, the fear of making mistakes is even greater. Normalize the fact that making mistakes at the beginning of a job is to be expected. Tell yourself that you have to make mistakes to learn. You might also state out loud to your new supervisor that you expect to be making some mistakes at the beginning. Stating it out loud makes it clear that mistakes are a normal part of getting acclimated to a new job.

6. *My supervisor tells me things in a blaming way. I feel like I'm bad, like I've done something wrong, and I want to shrivel up. How can I respond to this?*

Repeat what your boss said without the negative spin. "I hear you saying that....."

Acknowledge that your boss is trying to tell you something. Let her/him know that you cannot hear it when it is done in such a critical, harsh way. Can it be explained differently? Try to give an example of how it could be put so that you could respond.

Create a safe place for yourself to go inside as a way of getting through this moment. You may need to put some space between you and the situation, by saying you cannot be in the room and listen to blaming language and that you will come back later to have the discussion. Take time to regroup. Then think about how to approach your boss and ask for different behavior.

7. *When I hear or anticipate an angry exchange between people at work, I get anxious and want to get away fast. Is there a way to avoid feeling so scared?*

Take three deep breaths as a way of calming yourself.

Physically remove yourself from the situation. You are not needed there. Go to the bathroom or get a drink of water.

This is a time to draw on the safe internal landscape that you have previously created. In a psychic way, remove yourself from what is going on around you if you cannot physically leave. Have your own conversation with yourself. Repeat a prayer, mantra, or affirmation. Recite a poem. Sing a song quietly to yourself. Get the focus away from a situation that does not involve you.

8. *"I don't feel that I deserve a raise yet my friends tell me I do – how do I know when I am doing a good job?"*

There must be a saying somewhere that says, "Take the job that requires the most of someone and give it to a survivor." Seriously there is a strong tendency to be under-employed and overworked and to see that as normal.

Find a buddy, preferably at work, and together write down at least a page of responsibilities you carry whether or not they fit your job description (you can do this for each other). Think of accomplishments, things that you have done to make the department work more smoothly, results you have helped bring about, or ideas you have come up with for new systems, etc.

Think of new business relationships you have developed over time. Also think of how the department or the business is different in a positive way because you are there.

Watch your tendency to minimize

Do you know how many people simply do not know how to approach asking for a raise? This issue is not limited to the survivor community.

A little research will go a long way. You first need to know the standard industry salary for this position. Go to www.vault.com or www.salary.com to look at comparable salaries for your job. If you know someone in your industry in another company, ask that person the salary range for their position. Finally, create a document that gives evidence to support your request from the suggestions we just made. Edit it and have at least one other person read it for neutral language and over-wording.

When you determine that it's time to see the boss, set up an appointment. Don't let it happen spontaneously, even though your supervisor seems fine with that. You deserve a designated time. When you find yourself feeling smaller and smaller or ready to give up, take a breath. Put the smaller part of you behind you. You have an adult self that asks for things all the time. There is always a 50% chance of getting or not getting what you ask for. The authority in this situation will probably think more of you because you are showing courage, self-motivation and the ability to talk about hard topics. Practice your first two or three sentences in front of someone you know before you go in.

EXERCISE #5: A Hard Situation on the Job

*Recall and **write** about high stress situations that represent recurrent themes for you at work. If themes do not emerge immediately, take a few days to create a log – either at your current job or, if you are not currently working, then at home – of the various stressful situations you have experienced.*

Strategy for appropriate response.

1. *Brainstorm a variety of new responses with friends, a supportive person at work, therapist, sponsor, or mentor. (see Inventory #5: A Supportive Network, page 46)*

2. *Practice these responses as if they were scripts until they become more spontaneously available to you.*

Keeping Distractions at a Distance

Reminder: a trauma survivor can be hypersensitive to sights and sounds. There will be a tendency to be pulled towards exchanges and circumstances that can distract you and impact your ability to perform and focus on work. When this happens, your emotional responses are stimulated in reaction to these outside stimuli.

It is easy to hear an angry exchange or gossip and find yourself drawn in. Your eyes and then your attention and energy are directed toward situations that involve others. In addition, talking excessively with people results in a loss of focus and attention.

Begin training yourself to notice when you are being pulled into an outside exchange.

It takes time to learn skills and language that are both empowering and appropriate for the workplace. Practicing new responses will build a repertoire of tools to assist you in new situations. Eventually, these will become more spontaneous, natural, and effortless.

CHAPTER 5

Strengths Of Being A Survivor

Has it occurred to you that *because* you are a trauma survivor you bring special assets and attributes to your life and work? The following is a list of some attributes that survivors embody simply because they have overcome trauma.

Which of these descriptive words pertain to you?

❑ Courage
❑ Perseverance
❑ Resiliency of mind and spirit
❑ Heightened sense of listening and watching
❑ A quiet knowing

❑ Self-sufficiency
❑ Ability to empathize with others
❑ Attention to detail
❑ Good organizational skills

❑ Ability to take control
❑ Perception and insight
❑ Determination
❑ Focused attention on the inner life

More Strengths of a Survivor

❑ Spiritual perception
❑ Powerful intuition
❑ Ability to feel compassion and kinship with others who suffer loss, injury, grief, or injustice

❑ Strength and fortitude
❑ Sensitivity to conflict and danger
❑ Awareness of subtle imbalances
❑ Inner wisdom

❑ Heightened sensitivity or psychic abilities
❑ Sharpened discernment of how things move and change
❑ Ability to anticipate problems

❑ Ability to respond quickly to crisis
❑ A cultivated perception of what is beautiful, right, and true
❑ Humor
❑ Steadfastness
❑ Commitment/drive to health and healing

❑ Good at trouble-shooting
❑ Discrimination – observing first, not jumping blindly into a situation
❑ Resolve to keep going through difficult situations
❑ Empathy for people recovering and healing
❑ A commitment to growth and change

Other personal attributes you bring to work that increases your value.

Transforming Strengths into Transferable Skills

Consider how your strengths are transferable and add value to your workplace. For example, hyperawareness can be utilized in marketing and public relations to assess people's reactions to an idea you presented. A heightened sense of listening and watching to detect subtle reactions in facial expressions and body language are subtle skills. Perceiving a change in energy or a shift in attitude can be marketable in certain job functions.

Your goal is to acknowledge and transform your strengths into marketable skills. By claiming attributes and acknowledging valuable strengths, you are prepared, and are equal to other career and job seekers who are successfully shaping their worklives.

Never professionalize old, unhealthy coping skills.

Augment the list above with other authentic skills, personal attributes and talents. Ask coworkers, family and friends to provide feedback and add to your ever-growing list of attributes. You will have the advantage during the job search, in salary negotiations, at job performance evaluations and when asking for a promotion or a raise, of knowing how to articulate strengths and seize opportunities.

EXERCISE #6: *Identifying Personal Strengths and Attributes*

What strengths have you found useful at different times in your life?

In what ways have these strengths brought added value to your work?

It is essential to claim your strengths before you can present them in the work world with confidence. Which strengths do you claim as personal assets?

CHAPTER 6

Healing And Job Choices

As you navigate through the legacy of abuse, you will likely explore your personal history in deeper ways. It may become important to you to understand more fully the ways in which early childhood wounds affect you today.

Unless you are fortunate enough to take time off from work to fully engage in this exploration, you may be dividing your energy between emotional healing and performing at work. At times, healing while managing job expectations can feel overwhelming. It is unrealistic to believe that your attention, energy, and motivational levels can be sustained. This is an ideal time to adjust your expectations and to embrace a more forgiving and accepting attitude towards yourself.

Can you let go of rigid habits and adopt a balanced outlook during times of conflicting needs?

Consider letting go of:
- The notion that there is one "right" way to approach work.
- Individuals and groups of people who foster denial and who fear change.
- Identifying too heavily with your job persona.
- Negative thinking patterns; self-sabotaging behavior.
- Perfectionism.

79

Consider embracing:

- The knowledge that different levels of functioning are to be expected during the various stages of healing.

- A willingness to change the nature of your work in a way that supports your healing.

- A new model for the meaning of success while you are healing and beyond.

- Faith in your ability to be productive and achieve, even though you may be temporarily hindered while you are focused on your healing.

- A compassionate outlook on where career fits into your life while you are healing.

Reevaluating Work While Healing

It is appropriate to rethink your job or job function, especially when finding it difficult to manage the changes common to psychological and emotional healing while simultaneously responding to normal work expectations.

Staying in a current work situation can either facilitate or hinder healing. A current, familiar job can be important in keeping normalcy in your daily life. It provides structure and predictability. Daily contact with familiar people and known expectations are comforting.

Is it wise to stay in your current job?

Familiar job environments can be psychologically restimulating. Assess whether your job is providing a window to explore deeper issues and is conducive to your healing process. Talk it through with a supportive friend or your therapist. There are times when staying in a job is retraumatizing and has no healing value. Evaluate your job in terms of its value to you while exploring your personal history.

It may be an option for you to voluntarily downsize your workload if your ability to function changes during a particular time of healing. People can and often do create flexible job descriptions that reflect what they can reasonably take on and accomplish during different stages of healing. Some companies are supportive of their valued staff and want to ensure their continued employment.

It is not uncommon to leave a current position and choose an entirely different and less demanding job while focusing on personal healing. This type of voluntary downsizing may appear to be severe but provides not only continued income, but continuity and a feeling of worth. Choosing to downsize rather than struggling to perform as if your life was not in transition can be a healthy decision.

With a positive attitude, knowledge that it serves a temporary need, and having an understanding that it is meant to support you during a difficult period, you can have a positive experience and learn about interesting occupations.

Healing Stages And The Job Fit

Experts in the field of early childhood trauma have developed models for the continuum of healing. Most experts talk about three predictable phases survivors can expect to go through as they heal childhood wounds. Refer to our references at the end of this guidebook for books that can educate you about the expected stages of healing.

You have the ability to assess where you are in your healing process and understand what that means in relation to your capabilities at work. Evaluating your psychological state and honestly appraising your abilities will help you make appropriate job choices.

> *You can choose a job that corresponds to your level of functioning during various stages of healing.*

We have identified three stages to correspond with particular emotional states and capabilities and their impact on your work performance.

Remember, each person's process is unique. We hope you will use this section as a guide to educate yourself, to understand how profound the healing process can be, and to develop a compassionate and forgiving attitude towards yourself and your job expectations.

- **Memory Stage:** Peeling away the layers. Creating safety to explore childhood experiences in a deep way.

- **Recovery/Reentry Stage:** Integration. Making sense of the past and its relation to the present. Managing feelings and continuing to grieve the past.

- **Thriving Stage:** Reconnecting to life. Continuing to understand and work with core issues as they emerge. Letting yourself experience an expansive approach to the world.

The charts on the following pages delineate three distinctive healing phases, with associated capabilities, and their impact on work. These phases reflect a continuum of healing but can also fluctuate.

Criteria for Evaluating Work Capabilities

The Memory Stage

Internal and External Changes	Functional Capabilities	Impact on Work
Establishing safety.	Energy levels are low; the ability to concentrate is diminished; there is lack of focus.	Work affected by fatigue, a low level of energy, exhaustion, and the inability to concentrate.
Memories are triggered that resemble early trauma. Flashbacks or panic attacks can be frequent for some people.	Attention is directed towards self. The focus is on putting structure into each day.	Lack of mental clarity; difficulty learning new tasks.
Hypersensitivity and extreme emotional fluctuations are to be expected.	Capabilities are limited to meeting basic needs.	Feeling antisocial, especially at business gatherings.
Need to manage anxiety and despair.	Difficulty with thinking quickly.	Restimulated by co-worker's behavior or by certain physical surroundings.
Restlessness.	Likely to isolate and detach from people to feel safe.	Lack of interest in work.
Moving away from denial and validating feelings.	Fragmented and indecisive.	Can be vulnerable to scapegoating or being victimized at the workplace.
	Reactive/helpless.	
It is especially important to be compassionate and gentle with yourself and your emotions. Honor the need to focus on the emotional, inner world.	Need to protect self adequately.	Tolerance for noise and heightened stimulation is limited.
	Inability to access and act on inner strengths and resources.	Difficulty taking on more responsibility.
	Learning the need for stress management.	Absenteeism/lateness.

The Recovery/Reentry Stage

Internal and External Changes	Functional Capabilities	Impact on Work
Begins integrating healing and work.	Yearns to incorporate the wisdom of the healing process into a work setting.	Learns about physical and energy limits.
Integrates memories; continues exploration of woundedness.	Makes new meaning of childhood experiences.	Practices new communication skills on the job.
Learns new skills in boundary setting, self-care, and nurturing.	Deals with reality more comfortably.	Learns to be more assertive.
Focuses on relationships and learns healthier communication skills.	Observes and learns how others behave from a place of empowerment and mutuality.	Sets and achieves job goals.
	Is more tolerant.	Tolerates "gray" areas at work with more comfort.
Develops and relies on support systems.	Sees the positive attributes in self.	Increases self-advocacy.
		Completes tasks and meets deadlines.
Decides what and how much personal information to share.	Learns about boundaries; experiments with setting appropriate boundaries.	Understands the need for balance between work, home life, and relaxation.
Believes in personal rights.	Reconnects socially.	Learns and starts practicing healthy work habits and behaviors.
Lets go of old patterns and life habits. Notices discomfort that accompanies this shift.	Seeks rapport with others.	Practices self-care while taking on more responsibility.
	Notices and manages feelings.	Acquires self-knowledge by exploring different job options and environments.
	Trusts inner knowing.	
	Sets small reasonable goals.	Experiments with making mistakes instead of needing perfection.
	Is less rigid with self and others.	
	Has strong interest in self-examination and insight into sabotaging behavior.	

The Thriving Stage

Internal and External Changes	Functional Capabilities	Impact on Work
The healing process reflects a heightened sense of self.	Present with self in a more comfortable way.	Confident about self and capabilities.
Reclaiming of the self.	Able to see opportunities and act on them.	Able to screen outside stimuli.
Self-acceptance and self-forgiveness.	Engages in high level intellectual functioning.	Works effectively with different kinds of people.
The future is hopeful with a promise of life integration.	Tolerates a range of feelings.	Understands that making mistakes is part of learning.
Striving for contentment, and spirituality.	Increases risk taking.	Handles both negative and positive situations with diplomacy and tact.
Actions reflect being more fully engaged in life and living in each moment.	Is creative and flexible.	Manages conflict and confrontation constructively.
Energy is freed up for a broader experience of life.	Able to manage the workplace rather than react to it.	Feels in control at work.
Negative thoughts are consciously redirected to a more positive attitude.	Works well in a team.	Strives for meaning in work.
Acceptance of experiences life offers.	Accurately assesses ambiguous situations at work.	Believes in talents and ownership of accomplishments.
	Strategizes and plans future career goals.	Achieves balance between work and personal life.
	Develops trusting and positive work relationships.	Perceives self as successful and worthy of job satisfaction and rewards.

85

Thinking of a new job, and knowing what jobs have reasonable expectations can be a challenge.

Paying attention to the internal and external shifts and the differences in competencies in the three phases of healing will naturally bring you to the question of what kind of work is appropriate during this huge transition period. Trying to think of a different type of work and knowing what jobs have reasonable expectations is impossible without some knowledge of the kinds of jobs that correspond to a wide range of functioning and responsibility.

We have developed listings of standard jobs and occupations you can consider where functioning expectations relate to the stages of healing developed for this book.

Browse through these lists. Let yourself entertain a number of these possibilities and allow them to be a stepping stone to other creative ideas for jobs that support your recovery and healing. We have seen many people thrive in unusual job settings and believe they grew from the experience. We hear our clients praise "recovery jobs" that gave them the opportunity to work in a way that facilitated their healing process.

> I will create a healthy working environment by
> shifting my perspective and expectations
> through knowledge and self-effort.

1. Memory Phase Jobs

Levels of functioning will require jobs with limited or no direct people involvement. Look for work with less responsibility, a light work load, low stress, mundane tasks, and a reduced or flexible work schedule. **The recovery/reentry jobs may be appropriate (see next page)**

- Auction assistant
- Baker
- Billing clerk
- Book store stocker
- Catering assistant
- Chair webbing
- Office equipment maintenance
- Construction worker
- Cook
- Counter attendant
- Courier or Delivery
- Custodian
- Database & Word processor
- Distribution & fulfillment clerk

- Driver
- File clerk
- Food checker
- Forest conservation worker
- Furniture finisher assistant
- Gas station attendant
- General maintenance and repair person
- Grocery store stock clerk
- Horticultural worker
- Hospital attendant
- Hotel housekeeper
- House cleaner
- Interior/Exterior house painter

- Insurance claim processor
- Janitor/caretaker
- Kitchen worker
- Library assistant
- Mail room clerk
- Medical records clerk
- New account clerk
- Nursery/farm worker
- Painter/sign painter
- Pest controller
- Photo processor
- Plant/flower caretaker
- Post office clerk
- Private household worker
- Restaurant delivery
- Safety monitor

- Security guard
- Shipping receiver
- Stock inventory clerk
- Store clerk
- Survey caller
- Taxi driver
- Telemarketer
- Ticket seller
- Traffic clerk
- Tree trimmer and/or pruner
- Truck driver
- Tutor
- Upholsterer assistant
- Usher
- Valet
- Wallpaper hanger
- Web researcher

2. Recovery/Reentry Phase Jobs

People often find success during this healing phase as individual contributors or in non-management positions. Volunteerism, internships, or apprenticeships can be highly rewarding and nurturing.

- Administrative assistant
- Ambulance driver
- Animal rescue league worker
- Animal sitter
- Bank teller
- Benefits clerk
- Bookkeeper
- Bookstore associate
- Broadcast assistant
- Car attendant
- Cashier
- Catering assistant
- Child care worker
- Companion
- Computer administrator or programmer
- Computer technician
- Concierge
- Construction worker
- Consignment store clerk
- Cook
- Consumer safety advocate
- Copy editor
- Courier or messenger
- Customer service representative
- Day care worker
- Distribution clerk
- Dry cleaner
- Educator
- Environmental health worker
- Event timekeeper
- Floral designer
- Fundraising assistant
- Geriatric aide
- Hair stylist
- Health care/ hospital worker
- Home health aide
- Horticultural volunteer
- Hospice assistant
- Hotel bellhop/ front desk clerk
- Inventory controller
- Job placement specialist
- Library assistant
- Mailroom assistant
- Manufacturer's representative
- Mechanic
- Medical assistant
- Membership solicitor
- Motor vehicle clerk
- Museum docent
- Narrator
- New business development rep
- Nursing aide
- Occupational therapy aide
- Park ride operator
- Physical therapy aide
- Postal clerk
- Production scheduler
- Proofreader
- Quality inspector
- Receptionist
- Researcher
- Restaurant host/ waitress-waiter- bartender
- Sales associate
- School volunteer
- Sheltered workshop trainer
- Stage technician
- Taxi driver
- Technician
- Telemarketer
- Theatre usher
- Toll collector
- Tour guide
- Tourist information clerk
- Transcriber
- Tutor
- Typesetter
- UPS worker
- Virtual assistant
- Zoo keeper

3. Thriving Phase Jobs

Thriving jobs can be a job where you feel fulfilled and feel a sense of competence. Jobs in the former two lists can be thriving jobs in and of themselves. It may also be a time for considering new occupations that present different challenges.

New Roles

- Management
- Entrepreneur
- Leadership positions
- Specialist
- Small business ownership

- Self-employment
- Dual career
- Professional occupation
- Jobs reflecting interest area
- Program Administration

Scan through books at a bookstore under Careers to begin noticing your interest areas. Take advantage of career centers and seminars that promote diverse occupations. Consider seeing a career counselor who can assess natural skills, interests, motivators and values.

Write down the first action you will take to explore new job ideas.

Healing and Job Choice Assessment

Ask yourself these questions:

1. What is going on in my healing process and how is that impacting my work and my job choices?

2. How do you see yourself at work in relation to your healing process? (Refer to the chart of healing stages to honestly assess your capabilities at this moment).

3. How does this assessment help you decide which job choices will best correspond to your immediate needs?

4. Refer to the beginning of this chapter where we asked you to consider letting go of rigid patterns and embracing new attitudes to further support making job decisions. What attitudes will support you in this time of transition?

CHAPTER 7

The Job Match:
Criteria For A Healthy Environment

Choosing Smart:
Breaking Away from Toxic Work Environments

Choosing jobs is an opportunity not only to present yourself and your capabilities to a prospective employer, but also to evaluate whether the potential job and organization meets important criteria that you have established.

Many survivors of abuse hold the belief that they do not have the right to ask questions about the environment and working conditions or the scope of the job. In fact, it is not uncommon for people to accept a position without knowing the parameters of the job or having seen a job description. This is information you need to know to make an informed choice.

> **Job interviews are conversations -- two-way dialogues -- in which both parties find out more about each other.** They both evaluate whether the partnership would be a good match. As a job hunter, you have a right to ask any questions that will help you determine whether your needs will be met on the job.

In the rush to make a good first impression, trauma survivors disregard warning signs when choosing a job.

Have you fallen victim to any of the patterns below when making job choices in the past?

- Taking the victim stance; trying to anticipate what the employer wants and losing sight of your own goals.

- Exaggerating or undervaluing competencies.

- Underestimating the importance of the climate, culture, and environment.

- Making job decisions where you either overestimate or underestimate the responsibilities.

- Disregarding what your inner voice or gut tells you.

- Forgetting where you are in your healing process and choosing inappropriate jobs.

- Feeling powerless in the job search.

EXERCISE #7: Work Climate

In the space below, write two or three job titles you have had in the past.

EXERCISE #7: Work Climate (continued)

Develop a list of factors that hindered you from thriving on the job by looking at each position separately and asking yourself, "How did this environment make me feel diminished, undervalued, stressed, angry, or unable to do my best work?"

Choose four or five of the most significant factors and write them below.
    (Example: no control over the amount of work I am given.)

-
-
-
-
-

Now write a positive opposite term or phrase for each item above.
    (Example: I have input into the amount and scope of my workload.)

-
-
-
-
-

The factors listed above, have now become criteria that you will look for and ask about as you job hunt.

Using this criteria, begin to develop a list of questions to ask when you are job hunting.

(Example: can you tell me what kind of input the person in this position will have in determining the amount and variety of the workload? See the following page for more examples.)

_____

_____

_____

_____

_____

_____

_____

15 Questions To Ask When Choosing a Work Climate

- What is the nature of the work?

- What qualities are you looking for in your ideal candidate?

- What are the ways this company rewards people who do good work?

- Would I work independently or with others on tasks or projects?

- How often is overtime required?

- How do people in this group handle deadlines?

- What is the general atmosphere in the office?

- Is there one person who answers the phone for the group?

- Where would my workspace be located?

- What skills and attributes should someone have to manage this job successfully?

- Would I have an office with a door or would I be in a commonly shared area?

- When research is required, are resources located in the facility?

- To whom would I report and what is the chain of command?

- Will I be interviewing with the supervisor who oversees this position?

- What is the turnover rate for this job and why did the last person leave?

Reminder: it is important that you find a work situation that will value what you have to offer and also allow you to be safe. Make sure you see your workspace before you accept a position.

EXERCISE #8: *Criteria for a Healthy Work Environment*

Ask yourself the following questions to assess what constitutes a healthy work environment.

• *What do I need to do my best work?*

• *What gets in the way of doing my best work?*

• *What have I found in the past that helps me perform well?*

• *What detracts from my ability to function well at work?*

EXERCISE #8: Criteria for a Healthy Work Environment (continued)

• *What kind of work climate brings out the best in me?*

• *How much structure is important to me?*

Living The Job

When you choose a job you make the best choice and decision possible with the information you have acquired. The decision brings with it a commitment to carry out an agreed upon function for an established salary and set of benefits. But things change!

For example, the job description may change because of restructuring or a reduction in people to carry out the workload. It may be important to reconsider your decision and evaluate if there are ways to adapt or modify the situation. Remember, there is always an option to leave.

Always have an updated résumé available

Studies consistently show that successful professionals keep updated résumés and are always "window-shopping" for jobs. Some say that you should begin considering where the next job is as early as the first day of a new job!

Become exquisitely aware of the factors that come together to make this job work or not work for you. Know that a job is not contracted for life. There are always new decisions to be made. There are always fresh options to explore.

It's Never Over

Work is an organic process that changes from moment to moment. The successful worker will regularly reassess personal needs, wants, and priorities to ensure that the current situation is satisfying and productive. It can be valuable to evaluate whether your current position is the best place to be at the moment, or if another position would serve you better.

A great deal of information can be gained by watching other people carrying out similar and different jobs. Informational interviews and on-site observations allow you to find out from experts which skills are needed to successfully perform that job. This is how you become an "informed consumer" in the workplace.

"Window-shopping" affords you an opportunity to discover other available job options as well as providing a venue for ongoing self-evaluation.

You can know your job worth and value in the marketplace and investigate possibilities not previously considered. Implied in this process is the notion that you are taking responsibility for your career choices.

You can:

- Assess the worth of your skills and talents

- See where and by whom these assets are most valued

Remember:
- Window-shop

- Develop and hone skills

- Set sights on future jobs

CHAPTER 8

Thriving In The Workplace

Changing Expectations

"When I was in the reentry/recovery part of my healing, I thought I was thriving – I had no idea it could get better."

This statement from a trauma survivor expresses how remarkable it is to people who have known suffering and struggle to find that work can feel and be different. When you begin to make better choices for yourself, it is easy to settle for anything that seems better than what you had before. An abuse survivor knows too well how the workplace saps all the energy there is, leaving nothing for the other areas of life.

What is work supposed to feel like?

As career counselors and coaches, we are commonly asked, "What is work supposed to feel like?" "How do I know what is healthy?" The answers are not simple. It is not as easy as deciding what features you want in a new car.

Perceptions about work can change in an instant. Expectations about work are influenced on any given day by interpersonal exchanges, by what happened the night before, by your past work experiences, and by what you have learned to expect of work.

Reminder: ultimately, your expectations of work will change in a positive way as you:

1. Find out what you need and are able to articulate this information.

2. Seek out and learn about healthy environments.

3. Begin to make choices that better meet your needs.

4. Build on positive work experiences.

When you experience work as a place where you are valued, respected, and enjoy a challenging but reasonable workload, it will be natural to create a new, positive association with work.

Feelings Associated With Work

You can find many publications on worklife that perpetuate the idea that we should be in "bliss" at work – feeling "in the flow" each moment of the day. Strive instead, for the joy you will feel when you are in tune with your authentic self and can express your talents in your work. Bliss is a by-product of making every moment count. It is a direct result of learning how to thrive in the environment.

Expect to have a wide range of feelings associated with work, even when you choose the right occupation and the right environment. Typically, adults who have experienced the chaos of early trauma will expect to experience black or white feelings at work: an adrenaline high or boredom; heightened excitement or deadness; anxiety or numbness.

The terms peaceful, predictable, serene, comfortable, familiar, easy, and content, are not usually associated with or experienced at work. Creating a new dictionary of feelings is part of shifting from surviving to thriving.

EXERCISE #9: Feelings and Work

Write down the range of feelings that come up for you during the workday.

Add to your vocabulary of feelings words that depict ease, comfort, serenity, and inner peace. If words do not come immediately to mind, use a thesaurus to help develop a list.

Do you experience resistance to any of these words? If so, which ones?

What would change for you if you strove for different feelings at work?

Feelings of peacefulness and calm are part of a thriving worklife. Imagine how you would look as a thriver.

What Does A Thriver Look Like?

Thrivers are at peace with themselves. Thrivers are also energized. They exude confidence and a positive sense of self. Thrivers know they are part of the group; they are contributors; they bring creativity and flexibility to the work situation. They feel secure enough to inspire others. They are always looking for ways to improve their skills and the quality of their worklife.

Thrivers know how to see the gift in an awkward moment and make it work positively for them. Thrivers recognize and can express their talents and gifts. Thrivers help create a positive work climate. Thrivers attract other thrivers. Thrivers find time to help others develop. Thrivers have found balance in their lives.

Below are some elements we believe constitute thriving at work. Look through this list and see how many you currently possess or strive for at work.

Elements That Constitute Thriving At Work

- Maintaining balance between work and personal life.

- Integrating spirituality with worklife.

- Recognizing one's contributions and accomplishments at work.

- Feeling respected.

- Keeping on top of job responsibilities and expectations.

- Being able to handle difficult situations.

Elements That Constitute Thriving At Work (continued)

- Establishing realistic expectations at work.

- Feeling empowered.

- Feeling connected to and part of the team in the office.

- Automatically calling on grounding techniques when dissociation starts.

- Always searching for ways to make the atmosphere more supportive and nurturing for everyone.

- Having a support system in place to talk about hard situations that come up in the workplace.

- Being able to stay focused for long periods of time.

- Interviewing the company before taking a job offer to check for a healthy environment.

- Feeling supported by co-workers and boss.

- Asking for help when it is needed.

- Supporting self as well as others.

- Being clear with feelings.

EXERCISE #10: *Establishing Thriver Credentials*

Write in your own words how you look as a thriver. What are you wearing, how are you feeling physically, emotionally, mentally, and spiritually? How do people respond to you? What qualities do you bring to the workplace? In what ways do you positively impact your work world?

Who are the other thrivers in your life? Think of three people you see in your everyday life whom you experience as thrivers. Write down their names and describe what makes them thrivers.

1. *Name:*
   Description:

2. *Name:*
   Description:

3. *Name:*
   Description:

EXERCISE #10: *Establishing Thriver Credentials* (continued)

List one or two people who can be a model or mentor for you.

What can you learn from them?

How can you learn from them?

What do you want to ask of them?

NOTES

Let's imagine the thriver credentials in real time. Here are a few examples:

Thriver Example #1

You are attending some kind of meeting, be it a community meeting, a club meeting, an anonymous program meeting, or a meeting for work. You have learned how to dress appropriately for the type of meeting so putting your clothes together is quick and easy.

You arrive on time, or maybe a little early to chat with whomever comes first. There is an opportunity to help the presenter or facilitator with handouts and set up. You take advantage of that moment to ask if you can help. When finished, you chose a seat and relax, feeling calm and confident in yourself.

As the meeting progresses, you listen well, stay focused, and notice how you are feeling. You breathe when feelings come up. You are not distracted by your feelings. When judgments arise, you breathe and refocus on the meeting.

As a participant in the meeting, you think carefully through a remark or suggestion that would be helpful input to the goal of the discussion. You put the goal first rather than trying to make an impression or get attention with a comment that is more about you and less about the goal of the meeting. When addressed, you take your time in responding. If necessary, refrain from giving a direct response if you are feeling too anxious or overwhelmed.

When someone approaches you, the first feeling you have is interest and enthusiasm. You greet this person and ask something about them, creating a conversation and dialogue, avoiding the desire to talk about yourself.

Thriver Example #1 continued

At the close of the meeting, instead of departing quickly, you sit at your seat, slowly preparing to leave. If someone else has done the same, you make a positive comment about the meeting and what you got from it. There may be opportunity for continued conversation.

You notice judgments and see them as just that. You avoid forming an opinion about the group or people that is negative. Instead, there is a general feeling of well being.

Upon leaving, you have a feeling of being energized and peaceful. You take time after the meeting to integrate what happened and determine if there was anyone or any resource you wanted to follow-up on. You notate the action you want to take and the time frame desired to complete the task. You have been effective in taking every opportunity that the meeting had to offer.

Thriver Example #2

I have been assigned project manager for the latest office initiative. I am very excited. Even though I have doubts at times, I remind myself I have been chosen for this task due to my abilities and leadership potential.

I send a memo to each team member to ensure clarity of purpose and meeting times. I enclose an agenda for our first meeting and delineate responsibilities, project deadlines and milestones. It ends with a request for further suggestions.

At the first gathering of the group, I ask each member to share their vision of the project, explain their segment of the initiative and ask each person to voice any concerns they may have. We set the tone and expectations for the project.

We come to a consensus that I am to be a "task master" in order to keep each member accountable for their contributions. At the end of the meeting I pass around a comic I found poking fun at business people who had forgotten how to laugh. We all laugh about it and get the message.

As the project progresses, we take time to acknowledge our accomplishments and celebrate our milestones. Several times I am confronted by a team member, which immediately triggers me to question myself and my abilities. In response, I tell the person I will speak with them later in the day. I give myself the chance to regroup and reply with confidence.

109

Thriver Example #2 continued

As a group we take on the motto of welcoming each obstacle that arises as an opportunity to be creative. We brainstorm together on strategies to resolve problems and are proud of the ways we are able to create desired outcomes, using new and different methodologies than had been planned.

Several times I am the tie breaker and make decisions that do not have unanimous support. I talk to each team member to make sure they feel heard. We agree to disagree; the project progresses, and we meet our deadline with each team member feeling very proud of the results.

Embrace the belief that you have the right to thrive and flourish at work!

110

Now is the time for you to review this chapter's completed exercises and create your own personal thriver scenarios.

1.

2.

I will create a healthy working environment by
shifting my perspective and expectations
through knowledge and self-effort.

NOTES

CHAPTER 9

Taking It Forward

Throughout this book we have emphasized evaluating your needs as a survivor of childhood abuse. You will become a thriver by learning new ways to manage the workplace and taking an active role in shifting your expectations about what work can be. Each chapter has invited you to explore more deeply ways to shift your experience of work on a day-to-day basis. When you make a practice of using the material in all of the chapters in this book, the cumulative effect will propel you towards taking control of and managing your workplace.

As with any self-guided publication, you need to ask yourself, "What did I get from this book?" "What has been helpful?" "What are the parts that I want to take forward?" "Did this raise any issues that need further exploration?"

If you review the results of the inventories, exercises, and menus we have offered, it will become apparent that you more than anyone else, know what your own unique needs are, and that you have what you need to customize a thriving approach to your worklife.

> I will create a healthy working environment by
> shifting my perspective and expectations
> through knowledge and self-effort.

113

How To Take It Forward

Remember to come back to this book to assess your progress and refine your criteria for designing the optimal work environment. Pick a date six months from now to review the exercises and ask yourself how you have been able to apply/shift your perspective. Consider if there are new shifts you are ready to make to enhance your life at work.

This is not the time to quit!

Actively incorporate into your workplace what you have learned from this book. Consider the following suggestions to assist you in taking this practice forward:

- Choose a buddy – someone who is also striving to change an aspect of their life. Make a commitment to check in weekly or more often to evaluate and re-commit to goals. Notice any tendency you have to isolate yourself during the change process. Tell yourself that you do not need to do it all alone.

- Cut out or photocopy pages of this book that you find especially helpful. Bring them to work with you. Can you identify a visible location in your house to remind and reassure yourself that you are taking control of your life at work?

- Continue the integration of this book by creating visualizations or by designing a collage that represents your goals.

- Ask your therapist or counselor to help you put these tools and techniques into practice.

- Investigate our suggested reading list of titles that will assist you with your next steps.

- Create a support or study group with this book. Use the book, as a group, to set small goals that can be accomplished. Celebrate your accomplishments together.

• Set a goal that highlights some specific steps that you are going to take to effectively modify your experience of work. Write yourself a letter that sets goals and rewards. Mail this letter to yourself and specify a future date (no less than 4 weeks away) to open your letter.

Example:

Dear Self,

I have successfully completed the book *Thriving At Work* and am making a commitment to myself to assess ways to make my work environment a more nourishing and safe place for me.

I plan to pay more attention to how I sabotage myself at work and to look at and better understand my unhealthy coping patterns.

I will do a good thing for myself at least once a week and invite a person I want to know better to join me for lunch.

I will create a log where I can write down qualities that I have and I will keep this log near me at work.

I will revisit the exercises in this book in three months (date), to look at my efforts and accomplishments. I will give myself a reward of _____ for taking charge of my worklife.

Your Name
Date

Your Bill of Rights For Work and Career

I have the right to be seen, listened to and be valued at the workplace

I have the right to express my opinions and not feel threatened

I have the right to be respected by everyone

I have the right to receive training to do my job competently

I have the right to discuss concerns I have without being dismissed or be in fear that it will come back to hurt me

I have the right to ask for a raise or promotion based on the increased quality of my work or responsibility and ability to move to the next level, supported by documentation I provide

I have a right to ask for and receive appropriate supervision

I have the right to change my mind about a job because of the environment or an inappropriate supervisor. I can leave when it does not serve me to be there anymore

I have a right to change careers as I discover new things about myself

I have the right to express all of who I am in the workplace and my career

A Final Word

Creating the Worklife You Seek

The title of this publication, *Thriving At Work,* is a concept we enthusiastically advocate and embrace with tenacity. Those with a legacy of abuse are learning that they are so much more than their woundedness. Underneath the scars and pain, there is a person full of potential striving for solutions and answers to life's challenges.

Once the "cause and effect" dynamic related to a background of trauma is understood, one can begin to develop an awareness of when and how it plays out. A newly acquired response, based on the learning points of this book, is possible.

The effects of trauma or abuse.

There are some major "truths" that are common to many who have experienced one or more traumatic experiences in their lives. Each story is different, but the dynamics of how it gets played out in our work lives is often similar.

Trauma "survivors" many times feel guilt, shame and/or blame around having been victimized. These feelings can create self-doubt which leads to low self-esteem and a poor self-image.

From this place a belief system begins to form about being "flawed." As difficulties arise they are used as opportunities to validate feelings of inadequacy. A vicious cycle of negative self talk is engineered which diminishes self-regard and impedes effectiveness.

117

Survivors tend to be reactionary rather than proactive and respond to stressful situations in extreme ways. Some run and hide from confrontation trying to avoid it at all costs. Others are confrontational and sometimes bully their way through situations. Both extremes can be attempts at compensating, trying to cover up feelings of self-doubt.

There are common phrases that are heard from those who have a legacy of trauma, abuse, neglect, etc. "The devil known is better than the devil unknown," and "you can tell me how wonderful my work is, but I still feel like a fraud."

Experiences of trauma and abuse create deep wounds. They are like surgery scars. The wound heals, but the scar remains. Through the help of a good therapist, a willingness to change old patterns, a strong support system, and a commitment to do what it takes to heal from the deep wounding, the pain lessens and old coping mechanisms are replaced by new ones.

Eventually, the scar heals and no longer interferes with our life on a daily basis. Wounding becomes part of history. It does not define a person. We have had the opportunity to witness this change in so many of our clients and have been delighted to hear about transformations that have taken place for our readers.

With a new perspective, self-knowledge, support and the tools collected along the journey to heal old wounds, the quality of the minutes and hours of each workday can be increased. Gifts, talents, wisdom, wonder, light, enthusiasm, and compassion are available to offer the world.

NOTES

NOTES

EXERCISES AND INVENTORIES

Exercises

Inventories

SELECTED REFERENCES

Healing and Recovery

Bass, Ellen and Davis, Laura. *The Courage to Heal: A Guide for Women Survivors of Child Sexual Abuse.* New York: Harper and Row, 1988.

Berger, Leslie Beth. *Incest, Work and Women: Understanding the Consequences of Incest on Women's Careers, Work and Dreams.* Springfield, IL: Charles C. Thomas Publishers, LTD, 1998.

Blume, E. Sue. *Secret Survivors: Uncovering Incest and its Aftereffects in Women.* New York: Ballantine Books, 1990.

Bradshaw, John. *HomeComing: Reclaiming and Championing Your Inner Child.* New York: Bantam, 1990.

Carnes, Patrick. *Out of the Shadows: Understanding Sexual Addiction, 3rd edition.* Center City, MN: Hazelden Books, 2001.

Chopich, Erika and Paul, Margaret. *Healing Your Aloneness: Finding Love and Wholeness Through Your Inner Child.* New York: HarperCollins, 1990.

Davis, Laura. *The Courage to Heal Workbook.* New York: Harper and Row, 1990.

Herman, Judith. *Trauma and Recovery.* New York: Basic Books, 1992.

Miller, Alice. *For Your Own Good: Hidden Cruelty in Child-Rearing and the Roots of Violence.* New York: Farrar, Straus and Giroux, 1984.

Healing and Recovery (continued)

Napier, Nancy. *Getting Through the Day: Strategies for Adults Hurt as Children.* New York: W. W. Norton & Co., 1993.

Rich, Phil. *The Healing Journey Through Grief.* Hoboken, NJ: John Wiley and Sons, Inc., 1999.

Schenkel, Susan. *Giving Away Success: Why Women Get Stuck and What to do About it.* New York: HarperCollins, 1992.

Church Abuse

Bergeron, Gary. *Don't Call Me A Victim: Faith, Hope and Sexual Abuse in the Catholic Church.* Lowell, MA: Arc Angel Publishing, 2005.

Robinson, Rita. *Survivors of Suicide.* Franklin Lakes, NJ: New Page Books, 2001.

Sonkin, Daniel Jay, Ph.D. *Wounded Boys Heroic Men: A Man's Guide to Recovering From Child Abuse.* Avon, MA: Adams Media, 1998.

Job and Career Development

Americans With Disability Act (ADA). Contact: Job Accommodation Network, P. O. Box 6123, 809 Allen Hall, W. Virginia University, Morgantown, WV 26506-6123. (800-ADA-WORK)

Boldt, Laurence. *Zen and the Art of Making a Living: A Practical Guide to Creative Career Design.* New York: Penguin, 1993.

Bolles, Richard Nelson. *What Color is Your Parachute? A Practical Manual for Job-Hunters & Career Changers.* Berkeley, CA: Ten Speed Press, 2006.

Job and Career Development (continued)

Claman, Pricilla. *Ask... How to Get What You Want and Need at Work*. Boston, MA: Insights Incorporated, 2002.

Darling, Diane. *The Networking Survival Guide*. New York: McGraw-Hill, 2003.

Hayes, Kit. *Managing Career Transitions: Your Career as a Work in Progress*. Scottsdale, Arizona: Gorsuch Scarisbrick, 1996.

Murphy, Patricia. *A Career and Life Planning Guide for Women Survivors: Making the Connections Workbook*. Florida: St. Lucie Press, 1996.

Petras, Ross and Kathryn. *The Only Job Hunting Guide You'll Ever Need*. New York: Poseidon Press, 1989.

U. S. Department of Labor, Bureau of Labor Statistics. *Occupational Outlook Handbook*. Indianapolis, IN: JIST Works.

Weisinger, Hendrie. *Emotional Intelligence At Work*. San Francisco, CA: Jossey-Bass Inc., 1998.

Relaxation and Wellness

Benson, Herbert and Stuart, Eileen. *The Wellness Book: The Comprehensive Guide to Maintaining Health and Treating Stress-Related Illness*. New York: Carol Publishing, 1992.

Davis, Eshelman and McKay. *The Relaxation and Stress Reduction Workbook, 5th edition*. Oakland, CA: New Harbinger Publishers, 2002.

Kabat-Zinn, Jon. *Wherever You Go, There You Are: Mindfulness Meditation in Everyday Life*. New York: Hyperion, 1994.

Stoddard, Alexandra. *Living a Beautiful Life: 500 Ways to Add Elegance, Order, Beauty and Joy to Every Day of Your Life*. New York: Avon Books, 1986.

ABOUT THE AUTHORS

"Take what you have re-discovered about your true self and give it to the universe to blossom and bear fruit."
Nancy Brook

Nancy Brook, Consultant and President of Authentic Work, is a psychologically-based career counselor and coach. Background in behavioral science and vocational counseling led to the creation of a model of counseling that addresses the developmental issues related to childhood abuse. Nancy's model for career development integrates trauma theory, child and adult development, family systems theory, cognitive/behavioral principles thinking and vocational theory.

Known nationally for her expertise on childhood trauma and work, Nancy is a contributor to academic forums, and to professional development programs to the human resource and career management community. She promotes the importance of emotional and social intelligence for career success. As a certified emotional intelligence consultant, Nancy teaches, offers management enhancement coaching and speaks to international audiences on the subject.

Since the first printing of this book, Nancy has brilliantly navigated through treatment of breast cancer. She has written articles and papers on both trauma and work, and emotional intelligence. Her offices are in Boston and Southern Maine. You can reach Nancy at nbrook@authenticwork.com.

"Give yourself the gift of honoring the timing and direction of your process. Each step you take (big or small) allows the light within to shine brighter and brings you closer to thriving in your life."

Cynthia Krainin

Cynthia Krainin, is a Certified Professional Résumé Writer, Certified Job and Career Transition Coach, and a Certified Employment Interview Professional, group facilitator and lecturer. She is the career development columnist for an international magazine and has written articles for publications including the Wall Street Journal.

As President of Career Resources in Brookline, MA, Cynthia has made the process of changing jobs easier, more effective, and less stressful for clients around the globe since 1982. In addition, Cynthia works with HR professionals, business managers and educators in assisting their employees to increase personal effectiveness.

Overcoming the effects of past abuse and low self-esteem is the cornerstone of workshops, presentations, individual and group consultations that Cynthia presents. Her audience is made up of survivors of past trauma, as well as the professionals who work with them. She is currently consulting for the New England Shelter for Homeless Veterans, helping soldiers from past and current wars, overcome the past in order to meet the challenges of today's workplace.

Determined to lower the common statistics reporting that over 75% of Americans are dissatisfied with their jobs, Cynthia assists any individual or group wanting to upgrade their performance, career path and day-to-day experience at work. You can reach Cynthia at career_resources@verizon.net.